Written by Caroline Rowlands
Illustrations by Emiliano Migliardo

Every effort has been made to ensure the accuracy of the
information in the first edition of this book, published in 2024.

First published in Great Britain in 2024 by Red Shed, part of Farshore

An imprint of HarperCollins*Publishers*
1 London Bridge Street, London SE1 9GF
www.farshore.co.uk

HarperCollins*Publishers*
Macken House, 39/40 Mayor Street Upper
Dublin 1, D01 C9W8, Ireland

Red Shed is a registered trademark of HarperCollins*Publishers* Ltd.

Copyright © HarperCollinsPublishers Limited 2024
Cover typography based on designs by Thy Bui.

ISBN 978 0 00 864904 3

Printed and bound in the UK using 100% renewable electricity at CPI Group (UK) Ltd

001

A CIP catalogue record for this title is available from the British Library.

All rights reserved. No part of this publication may be reproduced,
stored in a retrieval system, or transmitted, in any form or by any means,
electronic, mechanical, photocopying, recording or otherwise, without
the prior permission of the publisher and copyright owner.

Stay safe online. Any website addresses listed in this book are correct at the time of going
to print. However, Farshore is not responsible for content hosted by third parties. Please be
aware that online content can be subject to change and websites can contain content that is
unsuitable for children. We advise that all children are supervised when using the internet.

This book contains FSC™ certified paper and other controlled
sources to ensure responsible forest management.

For more information visit: www.harpercollins.co.uk/green

If you love watching or playing football, you'll find TONS of fascinating facts in this fun-filled book...

Who is the fastest footballer on earth?

Which footballer signed a napkin as their first contract?

What does a dog called Pickles have to do with the 1966 World Cup?

Read on to find out the answers and lots more awesome information about the beautiful game!

Cristiano Ronaldo is not just a superstar on Earth... he's now part of the universe.

When astronomers discovered the 800-million-year-old galaxy, they were inspired by the Portuguese player's initials and shirt number and named it Cosmic Redshift 7, or CR7.

One of the reasons football clubs got rid of live animal mascots is quite a stinky one!

In the 1980s, football clubs began to swap animal mascots for humans dressed up in costumes to avoid all the unexpected poops on the pitch.

One of the strangest football mascots ever is Boiler Man.

The West Brom mascot belongs to a heating company that sponsors the club ... He certainly *warms up* the crowd on match days and has fans all over the world.

Only two goals in Olympic football have been scored from a corner kick... and Megan Rapinoe scored both of them.

The US player scored her first goal directly from a corner kick against Canada at the London 2012 Olympics. She then repeated the amazing feat against Australia at the Tokyo Games, held in 2021.

In 2023, French footballer Kylian Mbappé reached a record speed of 35.3km/h on the pitch.

That's not much slower than the sprinter Usain Bolt, who could reach speeds of up to 44.72km/h.

In 1921, the FA banned women from playing on FA-approved pitches.

They claimed 'the game of football is quite unsuitable for females and ought not to be encouraged'. How ridiculous! But that did not stop the players...

Teams like Dick, Kerr Ladies FC refused to give up and continued to play matches in parks and on rugby pitches.

In 1969, the Women's FA was formed with 66 clubs, and in 1971, the ban was finally lifted. Today, women's football is one of the most watched and played women's sports in the world.

When he was just 13 years old, Lionel Messi signed his first professional contract for Barcelona FC on a napkin.

The napkin was framed and is stored in a bank for safekeeping.

The first ever international football match was played at a cricket club and tickets cost just one shilling – worth about 5p in today's money!

In 1872, Scotland played England at West of Scotland Cricket Club. 4,000 fans turned up to watch and the result was a 0-0 draw.

A dog called Pickles saved the 1966 FIFA World Cup.

When the FIFA World Cup trophy was stolen just before the start of the tournament, the police went on a wild goose chase searching for it. Luckily, Pickles saved the day by discovering it hidden under a bush, when he was out for a walk.

There are 20 teams in the Premier League. Each team can have 25 players and eight of them have to be 'home-grown'.

This doesn't mean they have to have been born in the UK. They just have to have played in English or Welsh teams for three seasons before they are 21 years old.

The average age of a player in the Premier League is 26.6 years old.

Ethan Nwaneri is the youngest to have played in the league. He played for Arsenal at just 15 years of age.

At 39 years old, Chelsea FC's Thiago Silva is the league's oldest player.

Only eight countries have ever won the FIFA World Cup.

Brazil has won the most, with five victories, and Italy and Brazil are the only teams to have won the FIFA World Cup twice in a row. In 2026, 48 teams will compete for the trophy to become champions of the world.

The first Africa Cup of Nations was held in 1957.

It started with just three teams but now has 24 countries in the main draw. Egypt has won the Cup a record seven times, Cameroon has won it five times and Ghana has won it four times.

Henningsvaer Stadium is located in Norway, near the Arctic Circle, where the sun never sets during the summer months.

Thanks to the midnight sun, the stadium can be played on all night long!

A previous Chelsea FC manager and player is also a children's author.

Frank Lampard is not only Chelsea's all-time top scorer – with 211 goals – but after retiring as a player he returned to manage the club, and in between all of that he writes the *Frankie's Magic Football* series for children.

Lampard also has an IQ score of 150, only 10 points less than Albert Einstein and Bill Gates!

An ex-Arsenal goalkeeper now has his own YouTube channel.

Petr Čech entertains his followers by drumming along to songs by singers like Ed Sheeran and Rihanna.

Lily St Clair was the first woman to officially score a goal in the history of the women's game.

The Scottish player scored against the England women's team in 1881.

Johan Cruyff is regarded as one of the most creative footballers ever, after he reinvented the penalty kick.

While playing for Dutch team Ajax in 1982, he shocked everyone by passing his penalty to team-mate Jesper Olsen before kicking the return ball past a very confused goalkeeper.

Neymar da Silva Santos once got sent off for wearing a mask of his own face.

While playing for Paris Saint-Germain, Neymar celebrated a goal by putting on the mask, which was handed to him from the crowd.

The referee was not happy with this and gave Neymar his second yellow card of the match, which meant he was sent off.

Neymar gave himself the best birthday present ever in 2012, by scoring his 100th goal.

His team-mates helped him celebrate . . . not by giving him a cake but turning him into one! They covered the birthday boy with flour and sugar.

Neymar's 2017 move from Barcelona to Paris Saint-Germain made him the most expensive transfer ever – a whopping £190 million was paid for the star player.

After England lost the 1990 FIFA World Cup semi-final, England footballer Paul Gascoigne (Gazza) scored a hit record instead, about a foggy river in his hometown of Newcastle.

'Fog on the Tyne' reached number 2 in the UK charts.

In 1990, Gazza also became the first footballer to win the BBC Sports Personality of the Year award since Bobby Moore in 1966.

Only five other footballers have won it since – Michael Owen, David Beckham, Ryan Giggs, Beth Mead and Mary Earps.

One of the first UK women's football teams, Mrs Graham's XI, were met with riots when they tried to play.

Back in the 1890s, many men didn't like women playing football and would invade the pitch to stop their games.

The most goals scored by a team in the FA Women's Super League is 11.

Arsenal Women's Football Club achieved this record against Bristol City Women's Football Club, in Borehamwood, England, on 1 December 2019.

With over 160 caps for England and 26 goals, Jill Scott survived the jungle to be crowned winner of the TV show *I'm a Celebrity ... Get Me Out of Here!*

Did you know that Jill Scott's nickname is Crouchy (named after Peter Crouch)? Jill is 1.81m tall, almost as tall as Crouchy, who is over 2m tall.

One of the best teams in Europe is Real Madrid.

The Spanish side has won the UEFA Champions League the most times, with a massive 14 wins. The Italian side Milan has seven wins, and English side Liverpool has six.

Cristiano Ronaldo is the top scorer in the Champions League with 140 goals.

Lionel Messi is not far behind him with 129 goals, followed by Robert Lewandowski with 92 goals.

The captain of England's only World Cup-winning side was also the youngest captain ever.

In 1963, Bobby Moore became England's youngest captain at just 22 years of age. Four years later he got to lift the FIFA World Cup trophy.

Keira Walsh became the most expensive women's player when she transferred from Manchester City to Barcelona in 2022 for around £400,000.

Walsh joined her England team-mate Lucy Bronze, who also moved from Manchester City to Barcelona in 2022.

Most Manchester United fans don't live in Manchester or even in the UK.

The team is the most watched in the world and has over one billion fans globally.

Brothers Kolo and Yaya Touré are considered two of the best footballing brothers ever.

The siblings helped Manchester City win the Premier League for the first time during the 2011/2012 season.

When Côte d'Ivoire won the Africa Cup of Nations in 2015, the Touré brothers lifted the trophy together.

In the history of the Premier League, only three players have scored over 200 goals – Alan Shearer, Wayne Rooney and Harry Kane.

34 players have scored over 100 goals, including Frank Lampard, Andy Cole and Thierry Henry.

Richard Dunne holds the record for the most own goals.

He put the ball in the back of his own net ten times in 432 games. Oops!

Dunne is also one of the most sent-off players in the Premier League.

He holds the Premier League record for the most red cards – tied equally with Patrick Vieira and Duncan Ferguson.

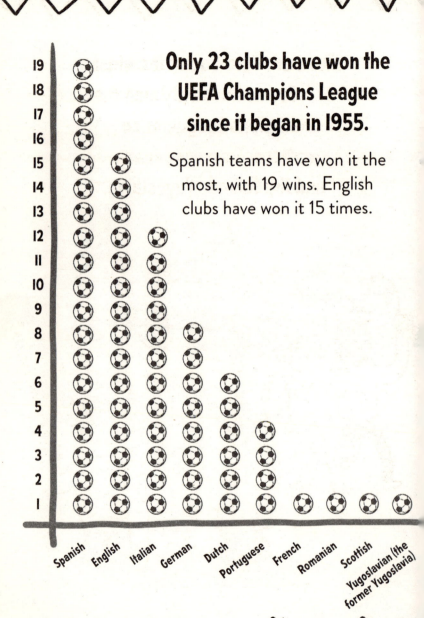

There are four countries whose club teams have only won the Champions League once – Scotland, Romania, France and the former Yugoslavia.

Asisat Oshoala is one of the best African women players of all time.

She has won African Women's Footballer of the Year a record six times.

The Premier League began in 1992 with 22 teams.

This was reduced to 20 teams in 1995 to make the league more competitive.

Only six clubs have always played in the Premier League.

They are Arsenal, Chelsea, Everton, Liverpool, Manchester United and Tottenham Hotspur.

Son-sational Son Heung-min is considered one of the greatest Asian footballers of all time.

The Tottenham Hotspur forward is also captain of the South Korean national team. In 2022, Son won the Golden Boot award, along with Mo Salah, for scoring 23 goals in the Premier League.

Christine Sinclair has scored more goals than any other player in the world.

The Canadian player has kicked 190 goals into the back of the net – that's 62 goals more than Cristiano Ronaldo has scored for Portugal.

In the 2003/04 season, Arsenal did what no team had done in 115 years...

They were unbeaten for the entire Premier League season, with 26 wins, 12 draws and zero losses. Even Chelsea fans had to agree it was pretty impressive!

The Invincibles were managed by Arsène Wenger and captained by Patrick Vieira. Arsenal forward Thierry Henry scored a whopping 30 goals for his club – the most in the entire Premier League that season.

It's easy to tell how many times a team has won the Italian league Serie A: count the number of stars above the club crest on a player's shirt!

The league follows a tradition where a team can add a star above its club crest when it has won the league ten times. Juventus FC has three stars because it has won the league over 30 times.

The Italian national side has four stars on its crest, as Italy has won the World Cup four times.

Lionel Messi was the top scorer in Copa América 2021.

He scored four goals in the world's oldest international tournament, which started between South American teams in 1916.

In 2015 Messi rejected the Copa América's Most Valuable Player award.

He did not want it after Argentina lost in the final. Argentina finally won the tournament in 2021 and Messi was very happy to accept and lift the trophy!

Some footballs are so hi-tech they don't need to be pumped full of air but charged, like a phone.

Made by Adidas®, the ball has a sensor inside it that measures things like speed and direction.

In 2016, referees made so many mistakes that the International Football Association Board decided to give machines a go – and agreed to a trial of VAR (Video Assisted Referee).

VAR is much stricter than human referees.

It was used in the FIFA World Cup in 2018 and 29 penalties were given . . . more than double the number given in the 2014 tournament.

One of the strangest goals ever was scored by a player's bottom.

Ben Watson managed to bump the ball into the goal with his behind. He scored this *cheeky* goal when playing for Cambridge against Notts County in the English Football League.

Ghanaian player Majeed Waris got his big break at the Right to Dream academy.

The academy is not connected to a professional team but it has produced seven superstar international footballers so far, including Mohammed Kudus and David Accam.

Carlo Ancelotti is regarded as one of the world's best football managers.

He has won the UEFA Champions League four times. Pep Guardiola has won it three times, and Sir Alex Ferguson and José Mourinho have each won it twice.

The 2022 FIFA World Cup saw 172 goals scored – the most ever scored in the tournament's history.

The 1930 and 1934 tournaments had the least goals – just 70 scored in each.

The FA Women's Super League (WSL) did not exist before 2011.

Eight players in the league have already scored more than 50 goals, but the Dutch and Arsenal player Vivianne Miedema is top scorer with 78 so far.

Only four teams have won the WSL since it began – Chelsea, Arsenal, Liverpool and Manchester City.

There are 12 teams in the league, all competing for the top spot.

In 2012, 11 players who graduated from the Barcelona FC academy played on the field at the same time, in a La Liga match.

Pep Guardiola, Andrés Iniesta, Xavi Hernandez and Lionel Messi all trained at the world-famous academy and went on to achieve footballing greatness.

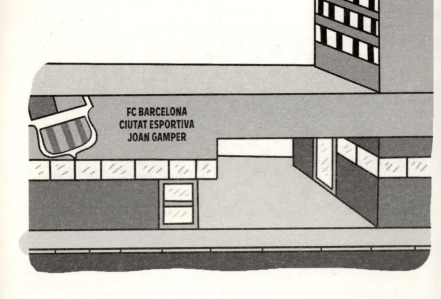

The most successful women's side in Europe is Lyon.

The French team have won the UEFA Women's Champions League eight times.

Lyon forward Ada Hegerberg is the all-time top scorer in the league – with 62 goals.

Ada also plays for Norway.

The Portland Thorns is the only team to have won the US National Women's Soccer League (NWSL) four times.

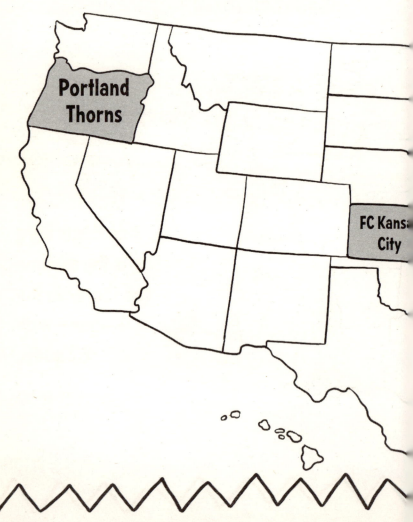

FC Kansas City and North Carolina Courage both tie for second place, with two league wins each.

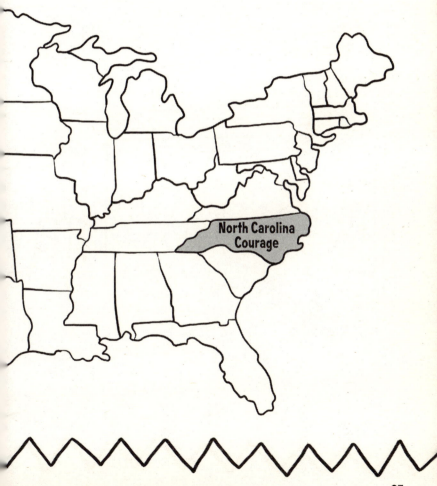

Scottish goalkeeper Jim Leighton once got substituted for another player because he lost his contact lenses.

He didn't have any spares, and without them, he couldn't see the ball clearly to stop it!

Roberto Baggio scored 86 per cent of all the penalties he ever took, yet he missed one of the most important in his career.

The Italian player hoofed the ball high over the crossbar during a penalty shootout with Brazil in the 1994 FIFA World Cup final, which Italy then went on to lose.

Forest Green Rovers FC is the greenest club in the world.

Their stadium in Gloucestershire has solar panels, electric car charging points, water recycling, an organic pitch and a vegan menu for players and fans. Well done, Forest Green Rovers – saving goals and saving the planet!

Two teams have won the UEFA EUROs more than any other.

Germany and Spain have both lifted the trophy three times. Italy and France have both won it twice.

Cristiano Ronaldo has not only played in the most games but also scored the most goals in the tournament – 14 so far.

Czech footballer Karel Poborský has the most assists in the tournament's history – eight to date.

Gerd Müller is the most successful player in the German league – the Bundesliga – with 365 goals scored.

That's a goal for every day of the year!

Polish footballer Robert Lewandowski came a close second with 312 goals during his time in Germany.

This does make Lewandowski the top non-German scorer in Bundesliga history, though.

Manchester United has very loyal fans!

In 2022, the club had the highest average attendances at its games – drawing bigger crowds than any other club in the world.

The best attended women's game in the UK was in 2022, with a record crowd of 87,912 fans.

They were watching England's triumph over Germany at Wembley Stadium in the UEFA European Women's Championship final.

The first women's FA Cup final took place in 1971 and was won by Southampton.

Arsenal has won the Cup the most times – with 14 victories.

Over 109,000 fans turned out to watch Manchester United play Real Madrid at the Michigan Stadium, USA, in 2014.

This made it the biggest football game in US history.

The largest attendance at a football game ever is believed to have been at the FIFA World Cup final between Brazil and Uruguay in 1950.

Almost 200,000 fans were there to cheer their teams on.

Jude Bellingham is one of the most promising players in the world.

The England midfielder was Birmingham City's youngest ever first-team player at 16 years and 38 days old.

Jude was also the youngest player to play for England at a major tournament and now, in his early 20s, he is playing for Real Madrid in Spain.

England first played in the FIFA World Cup in 1950, but did not do very well and lost its games against the USA and Spain.

England failed to even qualify for the FIFA World Cup in 1974, 1978 and 1994.

Scotland has qualified for the FIFA World Cup eight times, Northern Ireland three times and Wales twice.

Whenever the German league's biggest rivals, Borussia Dortmund and Bayern Munich, play each other, the match is called Der Klassiker (The Classic).

The two sides have met 109 times in the Bundesliga, with Bayern Munich winning 54 times. Borussia Dortmund has won 25 times and there have been 30 draws.

The Bundesliga began in 1963 with 16 teams. It now has 18 teams and Bayern Munich has won more than half (33) of the 60 titles.

György Szepesi was the greatest football commentator of all time.

Born in Hungary in 1922, he covered 14 FIFA World Cups and 15 Olympic Games, and he was still reporting six decades (that's 60 years) after his first commentary!

The most valuable player in the Premier League is worth over £150 million.

Erling Haaland plays for Manchester City and holds the record for the most goals scored in a single season – 36!

England players Jack and Bobby Charlton were not the first (or the only) brothers to have lifted the FIFA World Cup together.

The dynamic duo were on the winning England side in 1966, but West Germany's Fritz and Ottmar Walter played together and won the tournament for their team in 1954.

The Australia and Chelsea player Sam Kerr has scored the most goals EVER in the National Women's Soccer League (NWSL). Her record stands at 77 goals.

In 2019, Kerr also became the first Australian player (male or female) to score a hat-trick at a FIFA World Cup tournament.

Kerr scored for Chelsea in the FA Cup final in 2023 – winning it for the third time in a row.

Josef Bican is one of the greatest goal scorers of all time, but most people have never heard of him.

With 805 goals in 530 games, Josef had an average of 1.52 goals per game. This amazing, but mostly unknown, striker played for Austria and the former Czechoslovakia in the 1930s.

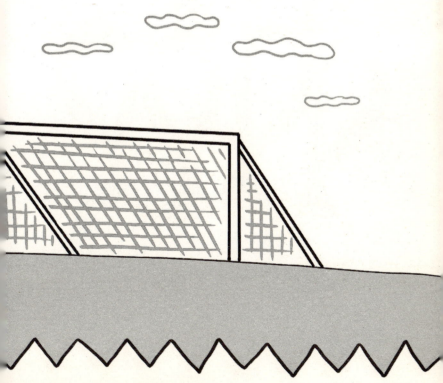

The Spanish women's national team is now ranked no. 1 in the world by FIFA.

The US team had held this top spot for the previous five years.

The US team has also won two World Cups, in 1991 and 1999, and four Olympic gold medals, in 1996, 2004, 2008 and 2012.

The most expensive season ticket for the Premier League 2023/24 season was for Fulham and cost over £3,000!

German and Italian fans can watch top teams like Borussia Dortmund and AC Milan for less than half the price.

The Scottish Football League was formed in 1830 and there are 12 teams in the top division, the Premiership.

Celtic has the biggest stadium, which can seat over 60,000 fans.

The last time any club other than Celtic or Rangers won the league was in 1985.

Aberdeen were champions that year, but Celtic has won the league 53 times and Rangers 55 times.

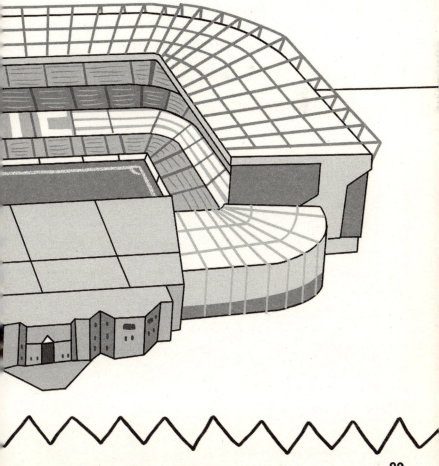

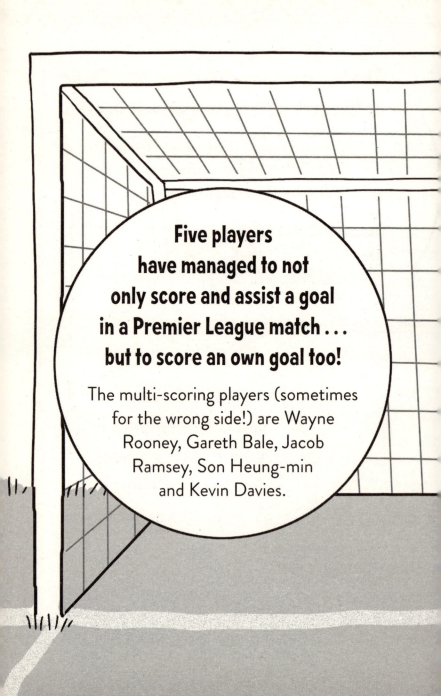

The UEFA European Championship anthem was inspired by music that was also played at King Charles III's coronation.

The anthem was written by Tony Britten. He based it on Handel's 'Zadok the Priest', written in 1727, and played at the coronation of Britain's royal rulers for hundreds of years.

Football is truly the king of all sports!

Look out for other books in the series!

Impress your friends with these matching name facts.

Arsène Wenger managed the team Arsenal . . .

Roberto Mancini managed Manchester City . . .

. . . but the best manager of all has to be Wolfgang Wolf who managed VFL Wolfsburg! Spooky!